How to Make Stocks and Soups with No Meat

- A Collection of Old-Time Vegetarian Recipes -

BY

S. Beaty-Pownall

British Library Cataloguing-in-Publication Data
A catalogue record for this book is available from
the British Library

Vegetarianism

Vegetarianism is the practice of abstaining from the consumption of meat – red meat, poultry, seafood and the flesh of any other animal; it may also include abstention from by-products of animal slaughter. Vegetarianism can be adopted for many different reasons. Perhaps the common motivation is respect for sentient life, and such ethical motivations have been codified under various religious beliefs, along with the concept of animal rights. Other incentives for vegetarianism are health-related, political, environmental, cultural, aesthetic or economic. There are varieties of the diet as well: an 'ovo-vegetarian' diet includes eggs but not dairy products, 'alacto-vegetarian' diet includes dairy products but not eggs, and an 'ovo-lacto vegetarian' diet includes both eggs and dairy products. A vegan, or strict vegetarian, diet excludes all animal products, including eggs, dairy, beeswax and honey. Some vegans also avoid animal products such as leather for clothing and goose-fat for shoe polish.

The term 'vegetarian' actually has a highly debated etymology. The Vegetarian Society, founded in Manchester, UK in 1847, says that the word *vegetarian* is derived from the Latin word *vegetus,* meaning lively or vigorous. In contrast, the *Oxford English Dictionary* (*OED*) and other standard dictionaries state that the word was formed from the term *vegetable* and the suffix

'-arian'. The *OED* writes that the word came into general use after the formation of the Vegetarian Society at Ramsgate in 1847, though it offers two examples of usage from 1839 and 1842. The 1839 occurrence is still under discussion, but the International Vegetarian Society's History group reported 8 other printed occurrences, prior to the Vegetarian Society's foundation in 1847.

The earliest records of (lacto) vegetarianism come from ancient India and ancient Greece in the fifth century BCE. In the Asian instance the diet was closely connected with the idea of nonviolence towards animals (called *ahimsa* in India) and was promoted by religious groups and philosophers. Among the Hellenes, Egyptians and others, it had medical or Ritual purification purposes. Indian emperor Ashoka was the first ruler to specifically assert protection to fauna however:

> '*Twenty-six years after my coronation various animals were declared to be protected... Those nanny goats, ewes and sows which are with young or giving milk to their young are protected, and so are young ones less than six months old. Cocks are not to be caponized, husks hiding living beings are not to be burnt and forests are not to be burnt either without reason or to kill creatures. One animal is*

not to be fed to another.' —*Edicts of Ashoka, Fifth Pillar*

Following the Christianisation of the Roman Empire in late antiquity, vegetarianism practically disappeared from Europe, as it was in other Continents, except India. Several orders of monks in medieval Europe restricted or banned the consumption of meat for ascetic reasons, but none of them eschewed fish. It re-emerged during the Renaissance, becoming more widespread in the nineteenth and twentieth centuries. In 1847, the first Vegetarian Society was founded in the United Kingdom, and Germany, the Netherlands, and other countries soon followed. The International Vegetarian Union, a union of the national societies, was founded in 1908. In the Western world, the popularity of vegetarianism grew during the twentieth century as a result of nutritional, ethical, and more recently, environmental and economic concerns.

Although many today fear that a purely vegetarian diet could have adverse side effects, especially from a lack of iron, it is actually very easy to plan healthy and balanced vegetarian meals. For the vegetarian chef, it is important to include the three essential food groups; protein (beans, lentils, nuts, tofu, soya), carbohydrates (grains, bread, pasta or potatoes) and fruit and vegetables. Some dishes, such as homemade pizza for example will contain all the food groups: cheese for protein, the base for carbohydrates and, for vegetables, the tomato and onion in the sauce, and vegetables in the topping. Making sure to eat dark green vegetables, such as spinach and broccoli, is important when planning vegetarian meals. Current scientific enquiry has now shifted from concerns about nutritional adequacy to investigating health benefits and disease prevention. The Academy of Nutrition and Dietetics have stated that at all stages of life, a properly planned vegetarian diet is 'healthful, nutritionally adequate, and provides health benefits in the prevention and treatment of certain diseases.' Large-scale studies have shown that mortality from ischaemic heart disease was 30% lower among vegetarian men and 20% lower among vegetarian women than in non-vegetarians.

Vegetarian diets offer lower levels of saturated fat, cholesterol and animal protein, and higher levels of carbohydrates, fibre, magnesium, potassium, folate, and antioxidants such as vitamins C and E. The practice has retained sustained interest across the globe, and in the current era of globalisation and increasing populations, many postulate that vegetarianism will only become more widespread.

STOCKS AND SOUPS.

BROADLY speaking, the vegetarian may enjoy almost every variety of soup, from the daintiest consommé to the most delicate purées and crèmes. But naturally they require special stocks. Roughly speaking, 1lb. of vegetables to one quart of water will supply a very good foundation broth, taking a full 8oz. of lentils, peas, haricots red or white, or the dried butter beans, to 8oz. of assorted soup vegetables and herbs, such as carrots, turnips, onions, leeks, a little celery, and a good *bouquet garni* (thyme, parsley, bayleaf, a scrap of lemon-rind), and, if liked, a *tiny* clove of peeled but *not* cut garlic. For the exact process I lift, with all apologies and acknowledgements to Col. Kenney-Herbert (Wyvern), the recipe he gives for such stock in his excellent work on "Vegetarian and Simple Diet," as it is the clearest formula I can discover : Wash one and a half pints of beans in plenty of water, removing all the withered and discoloured beans, etc., floating on the surface of the water. (It may be here remarked that haricot, butter beans, or peas are ordinarily used for this stock, though, when a deep coloured soup is required, red haricots or lentils should be chosen.) Let the beans soak, turning a plate over them to keep them under water, for twelve hours, then empty them with their liquid straight into a large stewpan, and bring this to the boil gradually over a low fire, skimming off all the scum that may rise, and throwing in a little cold water occasionally to facilitate this rising. When the liquid is clear, and the water is boiling, add the following vegetables, which should have been prepared and cut up whilst the beans were cooking : 6oz. each of onions, turnips, carrots, and leeks, 1oz. each of parsley and celery, ½oz. of salt, and a piece of muslin containing a bayleaf, a dessertspoonful of dried herbs (personally I prefer a bouquet of fresh herbs whenever procurable), and one peeled, but uncut, clove of garlic, and remember that it is a good plan to put these vegetable additions into a net, so that they can be lifted out directly they are cooked, for after this point they only weaken the stock by absorbing into themselves its aroma. All this cold stuff will throw the stock off the boil, so bring it gently back to boiling point, then draw the pan to the side of the stove, and only allow it to simmer very gently for two hours, or until the beans are perfectly tender. Now drain off the liquor, which is the stock required. The vegetables, beans, etc., should be set aside, after removing the herbs and the garlic and separating the beans from the rest. The vegetables will make either an excellent purée or a macédoine, whilst the beans come in for a variety of purposes.·

You may not be able at all times of the year to obtain all the vegetables given above, but onions are nearly always to be had, and you can make up the required quantity of the other vegetables by increasing the weight of those available.

This soup can be clarified exactly like ordinary soup. For instance, put the soup when cold into a clean pan, after carefully skimming off any fat, and break a whole egg into a basin with the whites of two more, beating them slightly together to break up the eggs but without allowing them to form a stiff froth ; pour this mixture into the cold soup, set the pan over a sharp fire, and stir unceasingly till it

comes just to the boil ; directly you see the first sign
of this draw the pan at once gently to the side, and
keep it at a bare simmer for half an hour, then
strain as usual. Thus made this becomes a very
delicate consommé, and may be garnished in any way
recommended for the ordinary meat consommé, only
of course without meat.

To make a specially good consommé you need what
cooks call "double stock," and for this you should
prepare some vegetable stock as above, then put into
a pan 2oz. of butter, or any good nut fat, melt this
over a moderate fire, then add in 4oz. each of carrots,
onion, and turnips, finely minced, 2oz. of leeks,
1oz. of celery, and 1oz. of parsley, all finely shredded ; let this fry sharply, stirring the contents of
the pan constantly throughout the process, adding,
as the vegetables begin to colour, three pints of the
warm stock ; bring this all to the boil, skimming it
carefully, then, drawing it aside, allow it to simmer
gently for two hours, after which strain off the soup,
reserving the vegetables, and finishing the soup as
before. A *very* little sugar dusted over the second
lot of vegetables, when frying, enriches both the
flavour and the colour of the soup, but this addition
requires great care, as, if in the least over-done, it will
give a coarse, disagreeable flavour to the soup.

Vegetable Stock II.—Another most excellent soup
can be made simply from vegetables, allowing a full
pound of mixed vegetables, and a bouquet to the quart
of water, in the following proportions : 6oz. carrots,
4oz. turnips, 2½oz. each of leeks and onions, and 1oz.
of celery. Mince the vegetables, put the onions and
leeks into a pan with a little butter till lightly coloured,
then lay in the rest of the vegetables with a dust of
sugar, a pinch of salt, and a little pepper, and fry these
all together for a few minutes; now moisten them with
two or three spoonfuls of water, cover down the pan,
and let it cook till reduced to a glaze, as this makes
a clearer stock. Then pour on to it the right amount

of water for the quantity of vegetables used, bring it all to the boil, skimming it well; draw the pan to one side, add in a handful each of mushrooms and dried peas, and let it simmer gently until these vegetables are thoroughly cooked, but not "mashy," then strain and clarify as before, using white of egg and fresh vegetables. An even more economical form can be made by taking 10oz. of dried peas, 3oz. carrots, $2\frac{1}{2}$oz. onions, $\frac{1}{2}$oz. of celery or celery seed, and a bunch of herbs to the quart of water. Season to taste, and either fry or not, according to whether you wish your soup to be light or dark, and finish off precisely as before. If no soda has been used in the water in which vegetables, beans especially, have been boiled, this makes an excellent vegetable second stock.

Another very useful foundation for soup, sauces, etc., is *Plasmon Stock.*—Place 1oz., or three teaspoon-fuls, of Plasmon in a saucepan, and add to it gradually half a pint of lukewarm water, stirring it all the time; put the pan on the fire, and allow it to boil for two minutes. When cold this stock will look like thin, semi-transparent jelly, though it can be used for stock hot as soon as made. This stock will keep a day or two if treated like milk.

It is hardly necessary to enlarge on consommés, for once you succeed in making clear stock, either single or double, according to what you want it for, you can garnish it in any way you please, the soup of course taking its name from the garnish, as in the case of meat consommés. A specially dainty con-sommé can be made by using the double consommé made with red haricots or lentils to ensure the dark-ness of its colouring. Have your soup tureen very hot, and place in it a small saltspoonful or so of really good tarragon vinegar, pour the soup on to this, stir-ring it well together, and serve garnished with cubes of royal custard and shredded green tarragon. The secret of success in this is to keep the tarragon flavour as delicate as possible.

Next follows the purée, of which there are, of course, absolutely endless varieties, and of which the well-known *Potage Palestine*, or *Artichoke Soup, Purée Soubise, Potato Soup*, etc., are familiar to almost every cook ; though it must be admitted she seldom realises how much more satisfactory they are when made with either skim milk, milk and water, or even plain water, than with the stock for which she demands such quantities of soup meat.

The following recipes give some idea of a few perhaps less well-known forms of Vegetarian Soups. Remember, if you wish to serve a *purée* it should be sieved, whilst for the fashionable *crème* it ought properly to be wrung through a tammy, or crushed through a fine hair sieve, and reheated with a delicate liaison of egg yolk beaten up in cream, and; needless to state, its basis should be nicely-made vegetable stock, mixed with an equal quantity of milk. For household use, however, an extremely nice soup may be made (which in France is known as *Potage Purée*, of whatever it is made) by simply crushing the contents of the soup-pan fairly smooth with a wooden spoon or a potato-masher. For these latter household soups, which are required to be downright substantial, a spoonful or two of dried, grated cheese may be stirred in sharply just at the last, or the cheese may be handed round, grated, at table.

Potage aux Pignole.—Fry 4oz. of well cleansed and minced pine kernels with 4oz. minced onions, and 1oz. of flour, in 1oz. or 2oz. of butter, till just beginning to colour, then add by degrees enough milk (or milk and white haricot stock) to moisten it, say two and a half pints for the above quantities, stirring it all well together ; bring it to the boil, and simmer gently for half an hour until it thickens ; then rub it through a hair sieve, or wring it through a tammy, adding a tablespoonful of cream, beaten up with the yolk of an egg, with seasoning to taste ; add a garnish of cooked

French beans cut in diamonds, and flageolet beans, reheat it all, without allowing it to boil, and serve.

Potage Bonne Femme.—Fry 4oz. minced onion in 1½oz. of butter, without letting it colour, for five or six minutes or so, till fairly tender, then add 4oz. well-picked and washed sorrel leaves, 1oz. of chervil, and a nice lettuce, all finely shredded ; season with a good saltspoonful each of salt and caster sugar, and stir over the fire for five minutes more. Now stir in a tablespoonful of flour, and again cook for five minutes ; then moisten gradually with one and a half pints of milk and water (equal parts), and bring it all slowly to the boil, when you draw it to the side of the fire, and keep simmering gently but steadily for thirty minutes or so. Meanwhile, beat up an whole egg with an ounce of creamed or slightly warmed butter, then work in by degrees one gill of the soup, being careful to get it all carefully blended, for, if not, the egg white will curdle when added to soup, and spoil its appearance entirely. Have ready some bread sliced diagonally, arrange these slices in a hot tureen, pour the boiling soup on them, and stir in the egg liaison, adding seasoning to taste if wanted, and serve at once very hot. Of course, stock, either vegetable or meat, may be used in preparing this soup, but it really is not necesary, milk and water, or, if preferred, plain, separated milk being quite sufficient.

Remember, that the bread used by French cooks for soup, when not fried as croûtons, is alway cut in this way : take a good lump of bread free from crust, and cut off one corner, "on the cross," as one says of materials, and then slice down the rest on the slant, parallel to the first cut. Cut in this way the bread seems to disintegrate quite easily, blending with the soup, and not making its presence in any way markedly obvious. Other cooks slice down a roll, and crisp it in the oven, to lay in the soup tureen.

Soup à l'Oignon, Stanislas.—These two versions

were given me by an old French lady, who in a modest way was a thorough adept in all culinary matters, and herself a gourmet. But the recipe *must* be followed exactly, for the first time at all events, however strange it may sound. Remove the crust from a loaf, break it up, not too small, warm a little before the fire or in the oven, then butter these pieces, and either toast or crisp them in the oven, and set aside. Now cut up or slice three good sized onions, put them in a pan with 3oz. of butter, and keep shaking them till they are nicely coloured ; then put to them the toasted bread broken up fairly small, and keep shaking the whole constantly till the onions are of a rich dark brown (but not the least *burnt*) ; now add one and a half pints of boiling water, with pepper and salt to taste, watch it *just* reboil, when you draw it aside, and keep it simmering for half an hour. This produces a particularly light and dainty soup, which is said to owe its name to King Stanislas Leczinski, an ex-king of Poland, and a noted gourmand. The lady who gave me the recipe warned me most solemnly against using any really rich, strong stock instead of water, by way of improving it (and I found her advice was quite true when a cook, bent on improvement, made it with good beef stock, and utterly spoilt its flavour !), but she told me as a variation, to use instead of plain water the water in which haricot beans had been boiled. The ordinary white haricot bean stock given above might, there- fore, doubtless be used, but finding the original recipe so g od, I never allowed this to be tampered with.

———— *au Fromage.*—The same lady who gave me the last recipe, also gave me this one—a favourite amongst sportsmen in France. Peel and cut up fairly small three good sized onions, and cook them in about 2oz. of butter or good fat, in a covered pan for one hour, till fairly tender. The steam prevents their actually frying. Then moisten with one and a half pints of hot water, in which a cauliflower has been boiled, or the same amount of bean stock, or, failing either, of plain water; add some slices of bread, cut on the cross, as recommended for *Potage Bonne Femme*, together with pepper, and salt if necessary (the cauliflower liquid might probably be quite sufficiently salt), cover down the pan again, and simmer it all for at least an hour. Now crush it through a sieve (for household purposes this is frequently omitted), and just before serving add gradually a good spoonful of grated Gruyère cheese stirring this, however, rapidly into the soup to ensure its blending well.

Potage Julienne Maigre.—Cut up into even sized shreds carrots, turnips, and a little parsnip, with a small blanched onion (say 3oz. or 4oz. of the mixed vegetables for one and a half pints of soup), put them on in a pan with a good pat of butter, a little salt, and a dust of caster sugar; cover down, and simmer the vegetables for ten to fifteen minutes, according to their age, shaking the pan occasionally to prevent their sticking to it; then add some finely shred celery, and some lettuce leaves stamped out in rounds the size of a shilling, and let these cook with the rest for four or five minutes. After this, pour in the amount of water needed for the soup (remember this water must be *absolutely boiling* when added, or it will turn the julienne strips into little hard sticks), add pepper to taste, and simmer the whole for a full hour. Now add (if in season) one or two spoonfuls of green peas, a few French beans, or some asparagus sprue cut into lengths, and simmer for half an hour more. As you are about to serve it, add in a little bit of butter, the size of a nut, and serve at once. You may use clear vegetable stock instead of water if you chose, but the soup, if carefully made, is excellent with only water for a basis.

A very nice soup closely resembling French

Julienne Passée, can be made by rubbing the vegetables used in the double stock making through a coarse colander or sieve, and reheating it all in the plain haricot stock, serving it with little round croûtons of fried bread, the size of a florin, well drained, dusted with grated cheese, coralline pepper, and minced parsley. Of course, this is not a purée, nor, strictly speaking, a julienne, but it is a very good soup, above all in town, where the vegetables have lost their first freshness.

Brunoise Maigre.—Take vegetables used in preparing the "double stock," cut them into cubes, and cook them for a few minutes in a little stock with some butter and a tiny dust of caster sugar, till the stock becomes almost a glaze; then stir in the required amount of stock, say a full one and half pints, let it boil up, and serve with fried croûtons.

Potage Purée de Pommes de Terre, aux Tomates.—Melt 2oz. of good fat, then lay in a minced medium sized onion and 1lb. of well coloured tomatoes, cover down, and cook int he fat for twelve to fifteen minutes; next add three pints of bean stock, water, etc., according to what you have, with pepper and salt to taste. Now lay in four to six very mealy potatoes, peeled, and cut up small, the red part of a carrot, and a small head of celery, also cut up fairly small. Bring this all to the boil, then allow it only to simmer till the vegetables are done to a pulp, and sieve them. Meantime, fry some little *croûtons,* the size of a shilling, in $\frac{1}{4}$ oz. of butter, to a golden brown and crisp, when you lift them out, and keep them hot in the oven. Meanwhile, pour the purée on to the butter in which you fried the croûtons, let it just boil up, then pour it into the hot tureen, throw in the croûtons, and serve at once. If preferred, the croûtons can be made a little larger, and dusted with minced parsley and coralline pepper before putting them into the oven.

Mulligatawny Soup.—Fry a good teaspoonful of

curry powder in ½oz. or so of butter or nut fat (to remove the snuffy taste so often noticed in under-cooked curry), with two or three bay leaves, then add six or seven tablespoonfuls of cold, curried vegetables, previously sieved with one and a half pints of water slightly flavoured with tamarind pulp. Simmer it all together for thirty to thirty-five minutes, then lift out the bay leaves, and serve with plain boiled rice. Bean stock may be used instead of water, and half a gill or so of *cocoanut* or *almond milk* (made by in-fusing 1oz. or 2oz. of the freshly grated nuts in half a gill or so of boiling water) added a few minutes before serving is a great addition.

Purée Crécy.—Slice the red part from seven or eight large fresh carrots (do not use any of the yellow part, or it will spoil the colour); now melt a good piece of butter or nut butter, lay in the sliced carrots, salt them slightly, then cover down the pan and let them cook very gently over a slow fire, stirring or shaking them now and again until they are dry, when you add to them about one gill of good Béchamel sauce, and let it all reduce for two minutes. Now sieve it, moistening it as you do so with two parts of good haricot stock to one part cream, and finish off with a liaison of an ounce or two of butter, working this in in little pieces, adding the last one or two after lifting the soup from the fire. If preferred, one or more egg-yolks, beaten up in a gill of single cream or new milk, also make an excellent liaison. Serve with fried croûtons. A very good household Crécy can be made with only ordinary stock or water, and no cream, using ten large and very red carrots for three pints of stock or water, and finish off with a liaison of a gill of milk rubbed up smooth over the fire with a spoonful of flour; reheat, and serve at once. Unless a liaison of some sort is added to this soup it will granulate instead of forming a rich smooth purée, and look like dirty water with tiny atoms of carrot through it. It will also separate in this way if the sieve through which it is rubbed is too coarse or the supply of carrots too limited. Remember, that from the end of March to the end of May carrots are not in condition for making this soup properly.

Cauliflower Soup.—Have ready boiled, but not overdone, one large or two small cauliflowers, and reserve a few of the best sprays of the white part to serve as a garnish to the soup. Put the rest into a quart of bean stock, and cook for ten minutes or so till tender enough to sieve, return this purée to the pan with a little more seasoning if required, and the pieces reserved for garnish ; make it all very hot and use. If liked, one pint of the water in which the cauliflower was cooked may be added to a pint of milk, boiled up with a good bunch of herbs, and . then used instead of the bean stock. Fried croûtons and a little grated cheese are a great addition to this soup. In any case, save the cauliflower water as a foundation for onion soup if not wanted on this occasion, only presuming that the detestable British habit of putting a knob of soda in the boiling water has not been adhered to.

Purée de Navets et Tomates.—Chop up one onion and put it into a pan with 2oz. or 3oz. of butter or nut fat; let it cook covered down for ten minutes or so, then pour in a quart of hot bean stock or water, add pepper and salt to taste, a small bouquet (parsley, green onion,bay leaf, and a morsel of lemon peel), with four or five medium sized turnips, one small potato, and three very richly coloured tomatoes. Let this all cook gently till the vegetables are quite soft, when you lift out the bouquet, and rub it all through a sieve ; now return it to the pan, let it just boil up, and serve. It should be of a bright red and of the consistency of cream.

Crème à l'Oseille.—Pick over and remove the stalks from some good sorrel, well washing it in plenty of cold water, then take two or three large handfuls,

11

tear these up, and place them in a pan with 3oz. of butter; when this has melted and the sorrel is thoroughly cooked, sprinkle in a teaspoonful of potato flour or cornflour, and stir it all together for two or three minutes ; now add one and a half pints of white stock or water, as you choose, and a seasoning of salt and pepper, and let it all boil together for fifteen minutes. Beat up the yolks of two or three eggs in one gill of single cream, mix them with a cupful of the soup, previously allowed to cool for a minute or two, have ready some crumby bread, sliced across diagonally, pour the eggs, etc., on to this, then skim the soup, and lastly pour it all on the rest of the soup in the tureen. Watercress makes excellent soup in the same way.

Purée Conti.—Well wash 1lb. of lentils (those known in France as *lentilles à la Reine* are best) and put them in a pan with two quarts of water, a bouquet, an onion stuck with two cloves, a carrot, and a blade or two of celery ; let these all cook till tender enough to sieve, moistening with its own liquor, and then, after adding enough good vegetable stock, sieve it, and return it to the fire, with a little more stock if necessary (stirring it well now and again to prevent its catching), and let it all simmer at the side of the stove for an hour, in a three-parts covered pan; have ready some nicely cooked celery, stewed in stock, and place this, cut up into neat pieces, into the tureen, pour the soup over, and serve.

P. Condé.—Put into a pan 1lb. of red haricot beans, with two large or three medium sized onions, and two quarts of salted, cold water ; bring it all to the boil, then simmer till the beans are quite soft ; sieve the soup, and pour on to it two glasses of claret, allow it all to simmer gently together for twelve to fifteen minutes ; then finish off with 2oz. or 3oz. of butter, and serve with fried croûtons. If liked, this can be made with white haricot beans or flageolets, using, however, in the first case, milk instead of water if wished (the water in which haricot beans are boiled should always be saved, as it makes an excellent foundation for all the vegetable sauces and soups), or with ordinary white stock for the flageolets, finishing off the haricots with a cream and egg yolk liaison, and the flageolets with cream and butter, and a few drops of pale green vegetable colouring.

Crème St. Clair.—Slice two onions and two tomatoes, and fry these for twenty minutes with 1oz. of butter, togther with a lettuce broken into shreds, and a good bouquet; at the end of this time add in 1oz. of *crème de riz*, three sliced tomatoes, and two and a half pints of white haricot stock; bring this all just to the boil, stirring it continuously, then let it simmer gently for forty minutes; add, if necessary, a few drops of liquid carmine to bring up the colour (only be very careful over this), skim well, rub it all through a sieve; turn the purée into a stewpan, and stand this in the bain-marie till thoroughly hot. When ready, serve, garnished with cooked shredded lettuce, carrot, and turnip, adding, just at the last, an egg and cream liaison, and garnish with fried croûtons of bread sprinkled with grated Parmesan cheese.

Green Pea Soup.—Boil one quart of old green peas in two quarts of water till tender, then pass them through a sieve back into the water in which they were boiled. Stew in the oven in an earthenware jar one pint of young green peas with 4oz. of butter, the under part of a cos lettuce, three cucumbers (sliced, and the seed removed), ten small onions, a teaspoonful of caster sugar, and, lastly, a spray of mint. When tender, add these all to the pulped peas and water, and boil them all together for a little time; stir in at the last a spoonful of cream, and serve with a pinch of cayenne and a little salt. (When young peas are not too plentiful the stock may be made by boiling the young peascods at the first

instead of using old peas.) A delicious version of
this is made by keeping a few of the young green
peas back, then crushing all the rest with the lettuce,
etc., through a sieve, together with the original stock ;
just boil it all up, put in the young peas, and serve
with croûtons of cheese straw paste highly seasoned
with cayenne.

Vegetable Marrow Soup.—Slice down 2lb. of
vegetable marrows, and place them in a pan with
4oz. of butter, a teaspoonful of caster sugar, an
onion, a seasoning of white pepper, and half a pint
of water; stew it all together till quite tender, then
pass it through a hair sieve back into the pan; rub
a tablespoonful of cornflour smooth with one gill of
milk, then add this, and about one quart of milk to
the purée, and boil it all together for a few minutes
(taking care that it does not catch) till of the consistency of good cream.

Corn Soup.—Cook one quart of corn, cut from the
cob, in three pints of water till quite tender, then
add 2oz. of butter mixed with (stirring the flour and
butter over the fire till thoroughly blended) a tablespoonful of flour, and cook it all for fifteen minutes
longer. Just as you lift the pan off the fire, stir in
a well-beaten egg with a seasoning of salt and pepper,
and serve. If liked, this soup may be sieved, but
this is not necessary for ordinary use.

Potage à la Bourgeoise.—Slice down thinly two
peeled Spanish, or four large English, onions, and
two leeks; put these into a pan with 2oz. of butter,
melted, seasoning them with salt, coralline pepper,
and a teaspoonful of caster sugar ; fry them for
twenty minutes without allowing them to colour, then
add one quart of good vegetable consommé and the
hearts of two heads of celery (previously shredded
finely and cooked till tender in some of the consommé);
boil it all up together, skimming it carefully whilst it
boils, then add about a quart more of consommé and
pour it all into a hot soup tureen, sprinkling in just

at the last 4oz. of freshly-grated Parmesan cheese, and serve, handing round with it fried croûtes dusted with freshly-grated cheese, coralline pepper, and minced parsley.

Potage au Melon.—Peel a melon and cut it up into dice, tossing it all in a little butter, but without allowing it to colour. Then put it into a pan with the butter, a seasoning of salt and pepper, and a bunch of herbs, and cook till tender; now sieve it, add to it sufficient liquid (half milk, half vegetable stock) to get it to the required consistency, just boil it all up together, adding, at the last, a spoonful of cream, and serve garnished with fried slices of melon, and fried croutons.

P. Purée Mancelle.—Blanch and shell thirty to forty chestnuts, and stew them in about one gill of stock, with a little butter and a good bunch of herbs, till they are quite tender; then crush them through a sieve and moisten this all with sufficient good, dark brown stock to make it a rather thin purée; bring it to the boil, add one or two spoonfuls of cream, and send to table with fried croutons.

Crème Parmentier.—Bake six or eight floury potatoes, and crush them, with some butter, with a clean wooden spoon; then pass this purée through a hair sieve (or a wire one for ordinary occasions), moistening it gradually with sufficient white or colourless stock to bring it to the desired consistency; reheat, and finish off with a liaison, of either two egg yolks beaten up with three or four spoonfuls of cream, or a little cream and fresh butter stirred in just at the last, before serving. This can be served with any garnish.

Purée Dubarry.—Break two or three good cauliflowers up into little bunches, trimming the stalks carefully, and blanch them. Have ready one and a half gills of boiling Béchamel, lay in the cauliflower, bring it to boiling point again, then draw on one side, and allow it all to simmer steadily for about twenty minutes until the cauliflower is quite tender. Pass it all through a sieve, moistening it as you do so with more or less rich stock, according to the occasion, season with pepper, salt, and a pinch of sugar, add a liaison of egg yolks and cream, and, just before serving, a small piece of butter.

Purée Grenade.—Cut into shreds ten or twelve large leeks, and stew them in butter till quite tender, seasoning with salt, pepper, and a dust of sugar ; then add to them about one gill of velouté sauce; allow it to boil quickly for a few minutes to reduce it ; moisten it with enough white stock, sieve it, and finish with a small piece of glaze, or two or three drops of Maggi's essence, and a dust of sugar. For household use it is very good if made with skim milk or ordinary second (colourless) stock, and finished off with an egg and milk liaison.

Haricot Soup.—Soak one pint of haricot beans for twelve hours in cold water. Meanwhile melt 1oz. of fat in a pan, then add one small onion, one small carrot, one small turnip, and a piece of celery, all washed, peeled, and thinly sliced, together with a bunch of herbs, two cloves, and six peppercorns ; fry these all together for five to ten minutes, keeping it all well stirred to prevent its burning ; now lay in the haricots, with one quart of stock or water, simmer till quite tender—for about one and a half hours— rub through a sieve, and reheat ; just at the last add a milk and flour liaison, made with one table-spoonful of flour and a half a pint of milk, and a seasoning of salt and pepper.

Purée Sans Souci—Soak 1lb. of haricot beans in cold water for twelve hours, then drain and put them into a pan with one pint of water ; simmer till quite soft and pulpy, stirring them occasionally, especially at the last, to prevent their burning ; add a very little more water as that in the pan evaporates, so that when cooked there shall be very little liquor left. Boil rather less than 1lb. of well-picked spinach in another pan, with a little salt, until tender, shaking it occasionally as it cooks, then strain it, and sieve. Pass the beans also through a sieve, and mix the two purées, diluting them to the desired consistency with a little unclarified vegetable stock, season to taste, add a small pat of butter broken up, and stir together over the fire till hot. Serve with fried croûtons.

Purée St. Germain.—Soak some dried peas for twelve hours, then drain them, and put them on in fresh water, cooking them slowly for five hours until the peas are quite tender; now sieve them. To each pound of peas, weighed before soaking, allow 4oz. of spinach which has been previously boiled and rubbed through a sieve; mix these two purées, diluting them with vegetable stock, season to taste, stir over the fire till hot, adding a large pat of butter, and when this is quite dissolved stir in, off the fire, one gill of cream, or, just before serving, lay in carefully some strips of poached custard. Send to table with fried croûtons.

The Italian dried green peas (*piselli verdi*, kept at most good Italian warehouses) are the most delicate for this soup.

P. Céléri.—Cook five or six heads of celery for a few minutes to soften them a little (or if quite young simply blanch them), then drain them, put them on with a little brown stock and a tiny pinch of sugar, and let them cook till quite tender; now rub them through a sieve, and moisten with a good gill of rich Espagnole sauce, then add enough good stock to bring it all to the desired consistency, sieve once more, reheat with 4oz. butter, a piece of glaze or a few drops of Maggi's essence, and a tiny grate of nutmeg. If liked, this soup can be made with milk or cream, and white stock, when it becomes a crème.

P. Velours.—Cut the red part from some carrots until you have altogether 8oz., and put this into a pan with 1oz. of butter, 2oz. of the white part of some leeks, and a pinch of salt; let it cook for five minutes, then add half a pint of well-flavoured stock, bring it to the boil, and let it simmer steadily till the carrot is quite tender, then pass it all through a sieve. Bring a pint of stock to the boil, and stir into it ½oz. of tapioca previously crushed up small ; stir this into the broth for five minutes, then cover down the pan, and let it all simmer together for twenty minutes, skimming it carefully now and again. Put the carrot pulp into a clean pan, and stir into it gradually over the fire the tapioca-thickened soup, and as soon as it is thoroughly hot serve. The success of this soup depends on its smoothness, so it must be properly and carefully sieved.

Scotch Kail.--This is an almost historic dish, and, though of the simplest, is decidedly appetising and hygienic, and at the same time economical. Well wash, pick over, and trim a full pailful of greens (*Scotticé*, "kail" or "kale"), then boil it in a good panful of boiling and well salted water for two and a-half hours till tender; now drain off the water thoroughly, and set this aside. Sprinkle a small handful of good oatmeal over the kail, and mash it all to a smooth pulp (it can, if liked, be sieved), then add a short half pint of cream, and as much of the kail liquor as will bring it to a nice consistency; season to taste with pepper (it should not want salt), watch it reboil, and serve at once, sending oatmeal bannocks to table with it. For the *Bannocks:* Put into a basin a large breakfastcupful of oatmeal, with a quarter of a teaspoonful of carbonate of soda, two tablespoonfuls of Albene, or nut fat, and as much boiling water as will produce a nice firm dough, working it first with a wooden spoon till cool enough to handle. Now strew the pastry board with a little dry oatmeal, and turn the dough out on this, dusting it all again with a little more meal. Next, with your knuckles, press it out again into a large round cake half an inch thick, then cut this cake into quarters, shaking off the loose meal as you lift it, and set it on a clean grid over a clear fire. When one side is toasted, turn the cake and toast it on the other, atfer which dry it for a little in front of the fire. Many cooks make oatcake in exactly the same way, only pressing out the dough as thin as possible, short of its breaking in the lifting.

Crème Cressonière (Watercress Cream).—Make a smooth roux with 2oz. each of butter and sifted flour, moistening it gradually with a pint of cold new milk, till it is very smooth and thick. Remove all the stringy coarse parts from some nice fresh watercress, and blanch this till it will sieve easily. Add a pint of this watercress pulp (which must not be too thick) to the roux, season to taste with coralline and white pepper and a little salt, strew in a little minced parsley over it and serve, handing round a boat of whipped cream seasoned with coralline pepper. This may also be served *en tasses,* in which case a teaspoonful of very stiffly whipped cream may be lightly dropped on each at the moment of serving.

————Cook three or four good market bunches of watercress in a quart of salted water, and sieve when tender. Make a roux with 2oz. each of flour and butter, and moisten with a quart of milk. Cook this till thick and smooth, and season to taste with coralline pepper and salt. Beat up the yolks of two eggs with a gill of cream, pour this liaison into the tureen, turn the boiling soup on to it, stir together, and serve with cheese pastry fleurons.

Fruit Soup.—A class of vegetarian food which abroad receives much attention, and is justly considered an important item in the menu, is scarcely recognised in this country, and this is fruit soup. Certainly we have the various kinds of fruit fools, somewhat akin to the fruit soups, but these are, from the amount of egg yolk and cream employed in their preparation, often too rich for delicate digestions. Fruit soups, on the contrary, are much lighter, and by careful preparation may be made to vary from a liquid that might almost be termed a fruit consommé to a substantial purée, which in not a few countries represents a notable factor in peasants' meals. In summer these soups are usually served cold, preferably iced, or chilled by being stood in or on ice till wanted,

For the clear fruit soup you use only the juice of the fruit (diluted or not with a little water as you please), to which the requisite substance is given by the addition of some starchy matter, previously rubbed smooth in a little cold water, and added to the fruit juice, just as the latter reaches boiling point, when it is allowed to cook till the whole is clear. The starchy matter may be either cornflour, arrowroot, sago, or tapioca; when using the two last, cook the soup rather longer than for the first, letting it all simmer gently till the sago or tapioca is tender, and all but if not quite transparent. When just about to serve, add a tablespoonful of strained lemon juice or of wine, as you please. The soup should be sweetened gradually during its preparation. Serve in china cups or glass custard cups.

For soft berries such as raspberries, etc., the method is a little different. Pick over, then mash about two quarts (or 4lb.) of raspberries with 1lb. of caster or granulated sugar. Let it stand for one hour, then sieve it, turn it all into a pan over the fire, and let it come very gradually to boiling point, when you at once stir in a tablespoonful of the usual thickening, previously blended with a very little cold water. When it is all smooth and of a nice consistency (about that of cream), add in a small tumblerful of sherry, white Rhine or French wine, or any other wine to taste. Lift off the fire at once, and set it aside to cool. Serve in cups and glasses set in crushed ice.

In Sweden, and indeed in other parts, the people prefer a really substantial soup thus :—Take one part of apricots or prunes to two parts of dried apples, and allow two quarts of cold water for each cupful of apples. Well wash the fruit, then soak it over night in the measured water, which should be cold. Next morning put the pan on the stove, with a cupful of either raisins or currants, or half of each, a dust of cinnamon or other flavour to taste (this is obviously a matter of individual taste), and one tablespoonful of sago or tapioca. Now add another quart of cold water, bring it to the boil, then simmer gently till it is all tender, seasoning it either with a little sugar or salt, as you please.

Another and simpler form of *apple soup* is this: Stew gently to a pulp sufficient apples to produce a pint of purée when sieved, sweetening this to taste. Add to this purée one tablespoonful and a half of sago or tapioca, previously cooked till tender and transparent in one pint of water. Now simmer this all for twenty minutes, flavour to taste with salt and cinnamon, strain and serve hot or iced, as you please.

Cherry Soup.—Cook some good, fresh cooking cherries in water in proportion to the soup required, some biscuit crumbs, and either a good grate of lemon peel or two to three cloves, until the fruit is cooked to a mash. Then sieve it, again bring it to the boil, and season to taste with sugar, red wine (do not let it boil after this is added), a tiny dust of salt and cinnamon. Hand round wafers or rusks with it. This soup can also be made (in winter) with dried cherries, mixing these with thinly sliced lemon freed from pips, etc., and a very little oatmeal, and is then served hot.

Strawberry Soup.—Cook finely-powdered biscuits in sufficient water (in proportion to the quantity of soup required), flavour it with wine, sugar, and cinnamon to taste, and, if the liquid be not sufficiently thick, stir in a little fecula, or potato flour, rubbed smooth with cold water. Or, if liked, use a little Plasmon stock. When well blended, stir in three or four saucerfuls of very ripe strawberries, previously marinaded for an hour or so in sugar and white Rhine wine; send biscuits and rusks to table with it.

Mixed Fruit Soup.—Take equal parts of strawberries, raspberries, stoned cherries, and, if procurable, bilberries, and crush them through a sieve after stalking them; pour as much water to them as you require for soup, and allow the fruit to cook very slowly for half an hour, after which sieve it all. When they have come to the boil, sweeten to taste, add a pinch of salt, a drop or two of essence of lemon, and as much fecula or potato flour dissolved in sweet cider as will make the soup the right thickness (about as thick as good double cream); mix in lightly at the very last the whites of two eggs, whisked to the stiffest possible froth, and serve this soup with either small plain biscuits or little bran-bread rolls.

These fruit soups are great supper and invalid dishes in Germany.

Lightning Source UK Ltd.
Milton Keynes UK
UKHW010650270121
377761UK00001B/198